AND HE'S *GONE!* MR. X HAS *JUMPED!*

PICKIN' 'EM UP LOUD AND PROUD, *DREDD!* THE STUNTER'S JUST JUMPED OFF SHOOTER TOWERS!

HE'LL FIND MORE THAN THE *GROUND* WAITIN' WHEN HE HITS *BOTTOM!*

SHOOTER TOWERS — AN' DON'T SPARE THE HORSES!

PARP!

...AND AS MR. X PLUNGES GROUNDWARD AT A PULSE-POUNDING 32 FEET PER SECOND PER SECOND, IT'S TIME THAT WE JOINED HIM —

HEY! WHAT GIVES?

THEY'RE CLOSING THE BAD-WEATHER DOME!

...BUT IT LOOKS LIKE MR.X HAS DONE HIS HOMEWORK!

IN JUST A FEW SECONDS WE'LL BE SPLASHING DOWN! SO STAY WITH US, VIDDERS, FOR THE LANDING OF THE CENTU—

GULP!

SPLUD

SPLAT

SHORTLY...

STILL ALIVE. MAYBE THAT'LL TEACH 'EM—

IN THIS CITY, ONLY JUDGES GET TO PULL THE STUNNING STUNTS!

REAL NAME: MARK FARMER
SOCIAL CATEGORY: ARTIST
STATUS: ACTIVE
CURRENT PROJECT: MOON KNIGHT/ALIEN LEGION

FAVOURITE RECORDS

1. Marvin Gaye: Let's Get It On
2. Chairman Of The Board: Salute The General
3. The Ohio Players: Honey
4. Parliament: Chocolate City
5. Was(Not Was): What's Up Dog?
6. Talking Heads: Naked
7. Curtis Mayfield: Superfly
8. The Undisputed Truth: Undisputed Truth
9. The Isley Brothers: 3+3
10. Nat King Cole: Unforgettable

FAVOURITE FILMS

1. Trouble In Mind
2. Raging Bull
3. The Duellists
4. The Godfather
5. Blade Runner
6. Rumblefish
7. Blue Velvet
8. Eureka!
9. Robocop
10. Stop Making Sense

FAVOURITE COMICS

1. Fantastic Four 45
2. Deadman (Neal Adams)
3. Swamp Thing (Bernie Wrightson)
4. Conan 24
5. Savage Sword Of Conan
6. Superman Annual 11
7. Silver Surfer 1-17
8. Daredevil 225-233
9. Dr. Strange Annual 1
10. Avengers Annual 10

FAVOURITE TV SHOWS

1. Bilko
2. Spitting Image
3. The Munsters
4. Match Of The Day
5. Cheers
6. Question Time
7. Only Fools And Horses
8. Horizon
9. World In Action
10. Arena

FAVOURITE BOOKS

1. Heroes: John Pilger
2. Books Of Blood: Clive Barker
3. In Cold Blood: Truman Capote
4. Will: Gordon Liddy
5. 52 Pick Up: Elmore Leonard
6. Night Winds: Karl Edward Wagner
7. Night's Master: Tanith Lee
8. Dark Companions: Ramsey Campbell
9. Nowhere To Run: Gerri Hershey
10. Malcolm X: Autobiography

ROLL ON
JUSTICE

21730

Story
IAN RIMMER
Illustrations
STEPHEN
BASKERVILLE

'Who are you?' growled Agostini at the wide-eyed kid who'd entered his workshop. Couldn't have been more than a teenager, Agostini thought. Small. Frail. Only spare flesh on him seemed to be on his round face. Hardly a threat, but a serious lapse in security for him to have got this far.

The nervy kid had started at the sudden question. His chubby cheeks reddened slightly. 'I'm Bond,' he answered tentatively. 'James Bond. Licensed holiday-cover mechanic.'

'You puttin' me on?' Agostini growled again. 'You don't look old enough, son. Anyway, where's Hailwood, the usual cover?'

'Got took sick,' James replied, still wary of the crabby, grease-smeared mechanic. 'And the others ahead of me at the agency – Surtees and Roberts – are on more important jobs.'

'Listen, son – ain't no more important jobs than servicing Justice Department vehicles and hardware,' huffed Agostini. 'Still, isn't your fault the agency don't see it that way. 'Sides, I got me a backlog of work stretching from here to the Cursed Earth Desert. I need help. Guess you'll have to do, James Bond. This way.'

'You, ah, recognise my name?' asked James, trailing the old, wizened engineer past several severely damaged Zipper Bikes. 'Mom was a video nut. She watched stacks of those cruddy taped movies from the Twentieth. Named me after her favourite character.'

▶

Agostini stopped to ponder for a moment. 'James Bond, huh? Never heard of him. Okay - let's see what we got here.' The mechanic crossed to a large vehicle, its shape lost beneath a heavy cover. 'Start on this,' said Agostini, unceremoniously dragging off the cover. James' eyes popped open wider than ever. He was staring at the road machine of the century. He was staring at a gleaming, pristine symbol of order. He was staring at a Lawmaster.

A Lawmaster... 4,000 cc of law enforcement; 500 brake-horse-power of crime buster; 48 kilos of perp control. It was two-wheeled justice dispensed at up to 570 kilometres per hour. It was fear, with a six-speed gearbox.

Calling the Lawmaster a motorbike was like calling its rider a policeman. It radiated authority and power, from the Justice Shield on the front wheelguard, to the tip of the twin exhausts at its rear. In between, the Notron V8 KT23 engine, silent now, waited to roar the rule of law through Mega-City One's streets once more.

James let his eyes rove along the 2.5 metre body. He'd hoped, dreamed, yet never really believed he'd one day be this close to the machine which he'd made his dissertation subject at Mechani-College. He'd passed the personality test that ensured that there was no potential criminal intent to his studies, but James had never had the chance to touch his personal metal and leather Grail before. Would he still pass that personality test. . ?

'Here's the report,' Agostini said, reaching for the large volume on the Lawmaster seat. He flicked through a ream of computer print-outs, punctuating his progress with an 'Uh-huh', or a 'Yeah', every so often. 'Well', he concluded, 'this baby's normally in the hands of Judge Dredd, but for now, it's all yours'.

The elderly mechanic then spotted the look of awed wonder that still adorned James' face. 'Hope you're payin' attention, boy,' rasped Agostini, thrusting the print-out into the hands of his star-struck junior. 'And don't go getting any crazy ideas. . .'

Agostini left the kid to the report and the Lawmaster. James sat on the former and stared again at the latter. He could see little wrong with its smooth, machine-tooled lines, save for a hefty dent on the front wheelguard, to the left of the Justice Shield. That must be what it's in for, James reasoned. For as long as it took to repair, the bike was in his charge – Agostini had said so – but straightening that guard would take him no time at all. James sighed heavily. And then he began to get a crazy idea. . .

 As he rocketted around Barry Sheene Block on the Lawmaster, James felt freedom for the first time in his life. The air sucked at his face, rippling his fleshy cheeks. The wind tugged and yanked at his hair, whipping it untidily about his head. But that was all part of the thrill for James – all part of knowing that, at last, he was truly alive.

That knowledge had first dawned when he'd realised he was going to take the bike. Once this intention was clear in his mind, the mechanics of the act were incredibly simple.

Starting the Lawmaster for someone with his knowledge of the machine presented no problem; but before that he'd had to disable the bike's Synitron Auto-Pilot computer. He didn't want some Judge riding a desktop terminal, transmitting a programme which would steer him straight to the Iso-Cubes. Keeping the main onboard computer turned off ensured there'd be no outside interference channelled through there. As he'd expected, bending the front wheelguard back into something approaching shape so that the wheel would turn unhindered took mere seconds. After that, it was just a matter of climbing into the seat, starting the engine, selecting first gear, and rolling out past the dumb-struck Agostini to wave goodbye.

Ever since, James Bond had been making the streets of Mega-City One his own. The bike handled like a dream, allowing him to stay in top gear, and at near top speed. Any vehicle in his way took immediate evasive action when he gave them a blast from the siren. And who needed to obey traffic signals when sitting astride a Lawmaster? As he left the residents of Barry Sheene Block inhaling his exhaust fumes, James reflected that he'd not even touched the bike's brakes yet.

He also reflected that he was living out a fantasy of modern man. He knew this to be true from some of those old videos he'd seen with his mother. Like the landscape flying past as he hurtled onwards, details were hazy, but his imagination had still been fired. Yes – he was Marlon somebody, in The Wild something. He was Peter Fondue – was that his name? – from Pale Rider. . . or was it Easy Rider? He was – no! On the Lawmaster, he was his *own* man. He was James Bond, razzing the living daylights out of the City. ▶

 'He's in one heap of trouble.' mused Judge Dredd when the communication came through. 'He's looking at 20 for stealing the bike – and double that with his traffic offences.'

Dredd was on foot patrol, marshalling a demonstration by the Simplified Spelling Committee, or the C.C.K. as they referred to themselves. The march was halted with little protest once the danger of a rogue Lawmaster was explained. It was heading their way, and everybody understood the words "motorbike victim" however they were spelt.

Dredd walked purposefully into the centre of the roadway, closed to traffic because of the march. He adjusted the transmit frequency on his portable communicator. He drew his Lawgiver, flicking its indicator needle to position three. Then he waited, while the demonstrators held their 'breff'.

 James thought about braking and turning back when he saw the signs saying 'Diversion: Roadway Temporarily Closed'. Instead, he opened the throttle even wider. This was a Lawmaster he was on, he reminded himself – a bike that diverted for *nobody*.

Moments later, James was bearing down on some makeshift metal mesh fencing stretching across the expressway ahead. Without hesitation, he hauled back on the handlebars and applied extra throttle. The 'wheelie' bounced the front tire into the fencing, which buckled, then crumpled under the bike's immense power. The machine's Firerock bullet-proof tires ground metres of meshing to dust before they once more bit the rockcrete roadway, allowing James to speed onwards.

The Notron engine's thunder echoed eerily along the expressway which James believed he had to himself. He was wondering if razzing an empty roadway would verge on the boring after what he'd already experienced, when he realised he wasn't competely alone. Ahead, in the distance, someone was standing in the centre lane.

 The sound of Dredd's voice booming at him from the bike's Likron communications unit was as startling to James as the words themselves. 'Hit the brakes, creep – or take a hit from a Lawgiver!' James suddenly felt uneasy for the first time since he'd mounted the bike. He'd stolen a Judge's bike, and there was a Judge directly ahead of him, clearly ready to administer the ultimate sentence. In a split-second, James had weighed up his options.

Stopping meant the end of the ride of a lifetime, and the beginning of a long, long stretch in the Cubes. To carry on, he'd have to open fire first. Triggering the bike's firepower wasn't a problem, but blowing away a Judge – with Justice Department hardware – would have drastic consequences for his own life expectancy.

What the hell, thought James, the ride's got to end sometime – even Lawmasters run out of fuel.

As he eased back on the throttle, James began to smile. So they'd take the bike back, slam him in an Iso-Cube for maybe half his life. So what? He'd always have his memories. He slipped in the clutch, dropped down a gear. What good was any thrill that you couldn't reflect on? Sure, he'd have plenty of time to reflect, but wasn't the point of any experience to remember the last time, and look forward to the next time? 'Roll on justice!' thought James. 'Me and my memories are ready to do time!' He floored the brake.

 Dredd watched impassively as the Lawmaster suddenly dipped. The perp hurtled over the handlebars and through the air, to smack bone-breakingly onto the rockcrete. He bounced, scraped and twisted along the expressway, while, behind him, the lock-wheeled Lawmaster did the same. Metal and leather stood up to the punishment better than flesh and bone, however.

James finally rolled to a halt a few metres from Dredd's feet. 'Same thing happened to me, last time I rode that Lawmaster,' the Judge informed the groaning, bloody, unnaturally contorted perp. 'Locking brakes was the main reason it was in with Agostini. . .'

 The medics did a fine job of putting James Bond back together again, so he could serve his sentence. Unfortunately, pondered James as he sat in his Iso-Cube, they hadn't done much for the incessant buzzing in his head. 'Wear a crash hat next time,' was the advice they'd given him. 'That way you'd still have those thirty six hours or so you've lost, because there'd be no severe concussion – and no incessant buzzing.'

James stared at the seamless, souless walls of his cell. The mystery of his imprisonment in the Iso-Cubes was equalled only by that last, perplexing remark from the medics. What could he have done, he asked himself, that should have necessitated wearing a crash hat. . ? ●

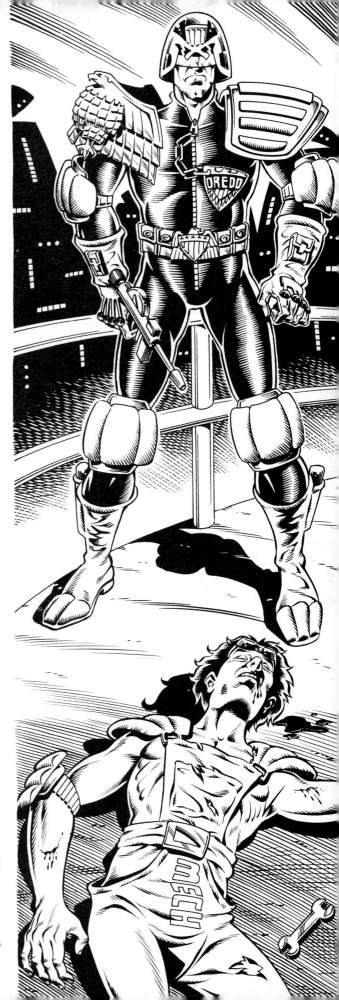

REAL NAME: RON SMITH
SOCIAL CATEGORY: ARTIST
STATUS: ACTIVE
CURRENT PROJECT: WILDCAT

FAVOURITE RECORDS

1 Hot Chocolate: You Sexy Thing
2 Iron Maiden: LP '66
3 Rolling Stones (The Lot)
4 Bessie Smith: The Heat
5 Harry James: Cherry Pink
6 Glenn Miller: In The Mood
7 Beatles: White Album
8 Atlantic Soul Classics
9 Danger Zone (Top Gun Soundtrack)
10 Woody Herman: Ten O'Clock Jump

FAVOURITE FILMS

1 The Man Who Came To Dinner
2 Midnight Cowboy
3 Dirty Harry
4 Jaws
5 First Of The Few
6 All The 007's
7 Bambi
8 In Which We Serve
9 Modern Times
10 The Graduate

FAVOURITE COMICS

1 Fantasie Comics
2 Zap Comix
3 Hotspur (1960's)
4 The Spirit
5 Rip Kirby (1940's, '50's)
6 Eagle (The Original)
7 Judge Dredd
8 2000 AD
9 Mask
10 Wildcat

FAVOURITE TV SHOWS

1 Wildlife On One
2 Flight Of The Condor
3 Till Death Us Do Part
4 Alas Smith And Jones
5 Timewatch
6 Bill And Ben
7 World In Action
8 The Two Ronnies
9 Everyman
10 Muppets

FAVOURITE CARS

1 Ford Model 'T' (1921)
2 Alfa Romeo, 2000 Spider
3 Bentley Saloon (1952)
4 Bristol 406
5 Cadillac Coupé
6 Lancia Appia G.T.E.
7 Lotus Eleven
8 Rover 3.5 (1980)
9 Maserati 5000 G.T.
10 Triumph T.R.7

JUDGE DREDD

ERROR OF JUDGEMENT

IN MEGA-CITY ONE'S GRAND HALL OF JUSTICE, CHIEF JUDGE McGRUDER CONVENES A DISCIPLINARY HEARING –

JUDGE DREDD, YOU STAND ACCUSED OF AN ASSAULT UPON A FELLOW OFFICER. HOW DO YOU PLEAD?

GUILTY.

I'VE GOT NO EXCUSES. I LOST MY TEMPER – SIMPLE AS THAT.

CHIEF JUDGE, I PROTEST. THIS IS A SERIOUS CHARGE. DREDD CAUSED ME ACTUAL BODILY HARM! THIS HEARING SHOULD BE HELD BEFORE THE FULL COUNCIL OF FIVE.

PROTEST NOTED, WINSLOW, BUT OVERRULED. IN MY JUDGEMENT IT'S PURELY A MATTER OF INTERNAL DISCIPLINE.

DREDD, DO YOU HAVE AN EXPLANATION FOR YOUR BEHAVIOUR?

THAT'S NOT GOOD ENOUGH! WHEN A JUDGE OF YOUR CALIBRE GOES OFF THE RAILS I WANT TO KNOW WHY. I INSIST ON IT.

VERY WELL, IF YOU INSIST...

IT HAPPENED ABOUT A MONTH AGO. I WAS ON ROUTINE PATROL IN BOB DURAN BLOCK PARK. I CAME ACROSS A GROUP OF YOUNG JUVES IN SOME AGITATION...

SCRIPT WAGNER/GRANT
ART RON SMITH
LETTERING T. FRAME

AS YOU CAN SEE, IT DIDN'T QUITE WORK OUT!

BADD RATTEEE! BONNNEEE SMACKK!

SHE'S NOT OUR BONNIE AT ALL!

SEEMS HER BRAIN NEVER COMPLETELY RECOVERED FROM THE SHOCK — FAILED TO MAKE ALL THE RIGHT CONNECTIONS.

THESE WERE GOOD PEOPLE, CHIEF JUDGE. DECENT, LAW-FEARING CITIZENS.

GRUD KNOWS, WE SEE ALL TOO FEW OF THEM. MAYBE I WAS WRONG, BUT I FIGURED THEY DESERVED A BREAK.

"I TOOK THEM TO SEE DOCTOR ROUFF AT THE FULMAN CLINIC —"

HER BRAIN SIMPLY NEEDS TO BE STIMULATED INTO REPAIRING ITSELF. QUITE COMMON IN THESE CASES. WE CAN HAVE HER FUNCTIONING NORMALLY WITHIN A MONTH.

OH, DOCTOR, COULD YOU?

CERTAINLY! NOW HOW WILL YOU PAY? MEGAMED? PRIVATE CRIPS PLAN?

WE-WE HAVEN'T GOT MEDICAL INSURANCE, WE HAVEN'T GOT ANYTHING. AND WE CAN'T GET ANY MORE CREDIT —

THE CITY WILL PAY!

BONNIE MADE EXCELLENT PROGRESS, CHIEF JUDGE. IT WASN'T LONG BEFORE HER BRAIN WAS CO-ORDINATING PROPERLY. I WENT TO SEE HER BEFORE THE END OF THE TREATMENT...

AHH...THAT'S A SHAME. YOU UNDERSTAND, I CAN'T WORK FOR NOTHING.

CRUNKKK!

I'M SORRY. IT'S MY FAULT. I SHOULD HAVE LEFT HER THE WAY SHE WAS.

NO, JUDGE DREDD.

THE WAY SHE WAS, THAT WASN'T OUR BONNIE. IF SHE'D HAD TO STAY LIKE THAT... THEN IT'S BETTER THIS WAY.

"WINSLOW WAS WAITING FOR ME WHEN I CHECKED IN —"

DREDD! WHAT THE DEVIL'S THE MEANING OF THIS? 130,000 CREDITS FOR MEDICAL EXPENSES?

IT'S WITHIN MY DISCRETION, WINSLOW.

DISCRETION'S ONE THING, DREDD — THIS IS SHEER EXTRAVAGANCE! AND WHY — ?

LEAVE IT, WINSLOW. I'M NOT IN THE MOOD.

SO SOME NO-ACCOUNT JUVE CAN GET TREATMENT! ANOTHER LEECH, FEEDING OFF THE CITY!

I SAID SHUT UP!

22

"THERE, YOU SEE! A TOTALLY UNPROVOKED ASSAULT! I DEMAND THE STIFFEST PENALTY – TWENTY YEARS ON TITAN!"

"DON'T BE RIDICULOUS, WINSLOW. IT HARDLY WARRANTS THAT."

"JUDGE DREDD, CONSIDERING THE MITIGATING CIRCUMSTANCES, NO DISCIPLINARY ACTION WILL BE TAKEN AGAINST YOU. I AM CERTAIN THIS ONE BLEMISH ON YOUR OTHERWISE SPOTLESS RECORD IS PUNISHMENT ENOUGH."

"CASE DISMISSED."

"DREDD – BEFORE YOU GO, A WORD..."

"HMMPH!"

"JUDGE MORPHY CAME TO SEE ME THIS MORNING. HE SAID YOU'D BEEN VOICING CERTAIN... DOUBTS ABOUT YOUR JUDGEMENT IN THE BUNT CASE."

"ON THE EVIDENCE I'VE JUST HEARD, THESE DOUBTS MAY WELL BE JUSTIFIED."

"YOU SHOULD NOT HAVE LOST CONTROL AND HIT WINSLOW. BUT, MORE IMPORTANTLY, YOU SHOULD NEVER HAVE BECOME INVOLVED IN THE CRICKLE CASE IN THE FIRST PLACE. THAT'S WELFARE'S JOB."

"I KNOW THAT NOW."

"SO ALTHOUGH I'M NOT TAKING ANY ACTION AGAINST YOU, I MUST INSIST ON ONE THING..."

"...YOU MUST UNDERGO A PSYCHIATRIC EXAMINATION TO ESTABLISH YOUR FITNESS TO CONTINUE AS A JUDGE."

CONTINUED ON PAGE 65

A STAR IS DRAWN

HE IS THE LAW – and has been for a staggering thirteen years, nine of them in his own regular strip in the *Daily Star*. In his marathon tour of duty, *Judge Dredd* has notched up no less than five awards and, in addition to *The Star*, appears in newspapers in South China, New Zealand, Ireland, Australia, Malaysia, Thailand, Latin America and the U.S.A.! On the following pages we re-present the sixth *Judge Dredd* daily series, 'Vigilante', written by the regular team of John Wagner and Alan Grant, and drawn by Ian Gibson. Eyes right – the action is about to begin! ▶

JUDGE DREDD
IN VIGILANTE

NO DOUBT YOU'RE WONDERING WHY I BROUGHT YOU HERE. THE ANSWER IS QUITE SIMPLE...

322

YOU ARE HERE TO DIE!

THESE ARE ALL ANTIQUATED IMPLEMENTS OF EXECUTION. RATHER APT, I THOUGHT.

YOU THREE SHOULD CONSIDER YOUR DEATHS NOT AS AN ACT OF MURDER—BUT AS AN EXECUTION!

WH-WHO ARE YOU? WHY YOU DOIN' THIS TO US?

323

BECAUSE YOU JUVES ARE SCUM—VERMIN THE JUDGES SHOULD HAVE WIPED OUT LONG AGO!

WELL, THEY MIGHT NOT HAVE THE STOMACH FOR THE JOB—BUT I HAVE!

JOEHAN SEBASTIAN DIAZ—FOR CRIMES AGAINST THE DECENT FOLK OF THIS CITY, I SENTENCE YOU TO DEATH!

NO—

AAAAAHHHHHH!

FZZZK!

ZZZZK!

324

KLUNK DAVISS— FOR CRIMES AGAINST THE DECENT FOLK OF THIS CITY, I SENTENCE YOU TO **DEATH!**

D-DON'T DO IT, MAN!

325

WILLARD WOTTS — FOR CRIMES AGAINST THE DECENT FOLK OF THIS CITY, I SENTENCE YOU TO **DEATH!**

H-HEY! I RECOGNISE YOUR VOICE! I KNOW YOU! YOU'RE—

AAAGGH!

KLUUNGG

326

I... AM **THE VIGILANTE!**

MORNING. JUDGES ARE CALLED TO THE **MUSEUM OF DEATH**—

DOOR LOCK WAS SLICED OPEN WITH A LASER.

327

NO SIGN OF ANY STRUGGLE. VICTIMS WERE PROBABLY BROUGHT HERE AT GUNPOINT.

SO WHY GO TO THE BOTHER OF STAGING A TRIPLE EXECUTION?

RECKON SOMEBODY'S TRYIN' TO MAKE A **POINT?**

VICTIMS HAVE BEEN IDENTIFIED AS KLUNK DAVISS—WILLARD WOTTS—JOEHAN SEBASTIAN DIAZ— ALL PROMINENT MEMBERS OF ONE OF THE LOCAL JUVE-GANGS!

328

SCORPS, HUH?

SOMEBODY SURE STUNG THEM!

LOOKS LIKE THE MAKINGS OF A **JUVE WAR.** LET ME KNOW WHAT YOU TURN UP. IRVIN— MASSEY—CHUBB! LET'S TAKE A TRIP DOWN TO **REHAB!**

ATLAS STREET **JUVE REHAB,** WHERE YOUNG OFFENDERS ARE GIVEN HELP TO ADJUST TO NORMAL LIFE—

USUALLY WITHOUT SUCCESS

BOYS! GIRLS! STOP FIGHTING! THIS IS SUPPOSED TO BE A **FRIENDLY** GAME!

GET LOST, DIRTWAD!

PIRANHAS DON'T PLAY NOTHIN' FOR FRIENDLY!

26

ATLAS STREET, JUVE REHAB—

GBSON 330

THESE CREEPS PLAY JETBALL FOR KEEPS!

WELL, I'M CALLING TIME ON THEM!

BREAK IT UP, MEATHEADS —OR YOU'LL BE PLAYIN' YOUR JETBALL IN THE MORGUE!

JUDGES!

WHAT DO THEY WANT?

JUDGE DREDD! THIS IS AN HONOUR!

YOU ARE—?

WOLLISS WILLIAMS SENIOR JUVE REHABILITATION COUNSELLOR!

331

CAN'T YOU KEEP THESE JUVES IN ORDER, WILLIAMS?

JUST YOUTHFUL HIGH SPIRITS, JUDGE DREDD. THAT'S ALL!

YEAH? THAT WHERE YOU GOT THE HEAT BUMP?

THE MAN WANTS TO SPEAK TO YOU! GET DOWN HERE!

YOWW!

332

LAST NIGHT THREE MEMBERS OF THE SCORPS— DAVISS, DIAZ AND WOTTS— WERE MURDERED IN COLD BLOOD!

SCORPS— DEAD? WHO DID IT?

TELL ME, MAN, OR I'LL KILL YOU... THEN HIM!

333

YOU'LL DO NOTHIN', LOUDMOUTH!

BOOK HER!

THREE SCORPS ARE DEAD, AND I'VE GOT A STRONG FEELING SOME OF YOU ARE INVOLVED!

ANYBODY WANT TO SAVE US ALL A LOT OF TROUBLE AND START TALKIN'?

NO? THOUGHT AS MUCH.

ALL RIGHT— LIE DETECT 'EM ALL!

334

27

JUST ONE QUESTION, JUVE—YOU KNOW ANYTHIN' ABOUT LAST NIGHT'S KILLINGS?

NO—AN' EEF I DO, I TELL YOU NOTHEENG!

JUST ANSWER THE QUESTION, MOUTH!

LIE DETECTOR CHECKS.

OKAY— NEXT!

WHO'VE WE GOT HERE—ADOLF HITLER?

HEY DON'T KNOCK THE HELMET! THAT'S A VALLYBLE ANTIQUE!

DON'T GIVE ME ORDERS, CREEP!

WHAT DO YOU KNOW ABOUT THE SCORP KILLIN'? YOU IN ON IT?

N-NEIN!

LIE DETECTOR CHECKS. YOU'RE CLEAN.

THE MASS POLYGRAPH TEST ON THE ATLAS STREET JUVES PROVES NEGATIVE—

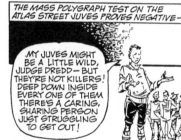

MY JUVES MIGHT BE A LITTLE WILD, JUDGE DREDD— BUT THEY'RE NOT KILLERS! DEEP DOWN INSIDE EVERY ONE OF THEM THERE'S A CARING, SHARING PERSON JUST STRUGGLING TO GET OUT!

YEAH?

YOU BELIEVE THAT, WILLIAMS, YOU'RE OVERDUE FOR A HOLIDAY!

OKAY— INTENSIVE INTERROGATIONS! FIND OUT IF ANYONE HAD A GRUDGE AGAINST THE VICTIMS—ANYONE WITH A REASON TO WANT 'EM DEAD—ANY BAD BLOOD BETWEEN THE SCORPS AND GANGS OUTSIDE THE REHAB!

2100 HOURS. NIGHT CREEPS OVER THE MEGA-CITY.

PSSTTT!

TARIQ ALLEY

YOU PIRANHAS!

YEAH? WHO WANTS US?

SNIK!

SNIK!

THE NAME'S VIGILANTE—

AND YOU'RE DEAD, SCUMBAG!

AAAGHH!

There's only one way to deal with the juve gangs, Pete. Exterminate them—wipe them out!

I have already made a start on this great task!

Are you telling us YOU'VE killed, Vigilante?

Executed, Pete—executed! The three scorp gang members who died last night—

I did it!

345

Tonight I executed another two juves—bringing the Vigilante's total to five. But they're only the beginning, Pete!

... only the beginning!

Get an immediate trace on that call!

Can you get a make on his voice?

No—creeps using a scrambler!

346

The Vigilante calls upon decent citizens everywhere—join me in my great campaign! Wipe the scourge of the juve gangs from our streets!

Thanks, er ... Vigilante.

CLICK!

Well, if anyone else has a point to make about the extermination of our juvenile population, or anything else, call line nine on nine-nine-nine-nine—nine-nine-nine-nine—

Nine!

Traced that call—it's coming from a pay booth on Lower Slone!

347

Control to Dredd! Check out pay booth on Lower Slone!

Masked raider identifying himself as 'The Vigilante' claims to have killed your three scorps!

On my way!

348

Control! I'm at the booth on Slone. No sign of your Vigilante.

He's left a message, though!

CHECK THE TRASH IN TARIQ ALLEY — Vig

Have forensic check the booth for prints. I'll be in touch.

349

30

CONTROL—I GOT TWO MORE STIFFS, TARIQ ALLEY.

GUESS THIS VIGILANTE'S OUR MAN!

350

EXAMINATION OF THE VID BOOTH YIELDS NO CLUE TO THE IDENTITY OF *THE VIGILANTE—*

THE TWO JUVES WERE KILLED WITH A LASER—COULD BE THE SAME WEAPON USED TO BREAK INTO THE MUSEUM OF DEATH ...

... WHERE THE OTHER THREE BODIES WERE FOUND!

CONTROL TO ANY UNIT, VICINITY PYRONE TOWER!

351

WE HAVE REPORTS OF GUNFIRE, TOWER WALK!

DREDD HERE! I'LL TAKE IT!

YOU STINKIN' JUVES! YOU'VE HAD IT YOUR WAY TOO LONG!

TODAY IS THE DAY OF THE VIGILANTE!

RIVET! RIVET! RIVET!

POK! POK! POK!

THE KOOK'S SHOOTIN' AT US!

352

DREDD HERE. PERP IN SIGHT— COULD BE OUR MAN!

IT'S JUDGE DREDD!

GO GET THAT MANIAC, JUDGE!

YOU!

THIS IS YOUR ONE WARNING— DROP THAT WEAPON!

353

DREDD

YOU STAY OUTTA THIS, JUDGE! WE'RE ON THE SAME SIDE! ALL JUVES ARE *EVIL*— THEY *GOTTA* DIE!

SO STAND ASIDE! THE VIGILANTE'S GOT A JOB TO FINISH!

IT'S FINISHED, CREEP!

354

355

AAAAH!

CONTROL— GET A MED·SQUAD TO PYRONE PLAZA!

WEEEOOOWEEEOOWEEE!

THE VIGILANTE, HUH?

LET'S TAKE A LOOK AT YOU.

YOU... SHOULDN'T HAVE SHOT ME, JUDGE... JUVES ARE SCUM! THEY... THEY DESERVE TO DIE! I ONLY DID... WHAT'S RIGHT...

356

THE OTHER JUVE GANG KILLINGS— THE SCORPS— THEY YOUR WORK AS WELL?

SURE... I KILLED THEM— DIRTY DELINQS! MUGGERS AND THIEVES— THAT'S ALL THEY ARE!

MAYBE SO... BUT YOU DIDN'T KILL 'EM, CREEP!

357

THE WOUNDED PERP IS TAKEN AWAY—

HE'S NOT OUR VIGILANTE!

NAME'S ED WINKEL. LIVES IN THE TOWER. HE PROBABLY SAW THE REAL VIGILANTE ON LINE 9— THOUGHT HE'D JOIN IN THE FUN!

COPYCAT KILLER... FIRST OF MANY, NO DOUBT!

YEAH— ONE CREEP IN A CAPE, AND EVERY KOOK IN TOWN COMES CRAWLIN' OUT OF THE 'CRETE!

358

0900 HOURS, ATLAS STREET JUVE REHAB—

THE VIGILANTE CLAIMED ANOTHER TWO VICTIMS LAST NIGHT— BOTH PIRANHA GANG MEMBERS, BOTH ATTENDING THIS REHAB!

OH MY GRUD! WHO?

CLUSKEY AND TURREEN.

NO! NOT SCARLEG AND SPIT! THEY WERE TWO OF MY NICEST JUVES!

359·

32

FIVE OF MY BOYS DEAD! **WHY,** JUDGE DREDD? WHY HAS THIS **VIGILANTE** GOT IT IN FOR US?

THAT'S WHAT I'D LIKE TO KNOW, WILLIAMS.

WE'VE CHECKED EVERY SUSPECT ON THE LIST—ALL NEGATIVE! THERE MUST BE SOMEONE ELSE — SOMEONE WHO HATES THE JUVES IN THIS REHAB ENOUGH TO KILL THEM

THINK, MAN!

HMM... I SUPPOSE ALMOST **EVERYBODY** HATES THEM. IT'S JUST A QUESTION OF **DEGREE!**

360

YOU SEE, JUDGE DREDD, MOST PEOPLE DON'T UNDERSTAND JUVE GANGS. BUT I'VE FOUND THAT IF YOU TREAT THEM WITH **KINDNESS** AND **RESPECT,** THEY'LL SOON COME TO RESPECT **YOU.**

BOINK! CRAAASH!

HEY, STOOPID! GIMME THE BALL BACK OR I'LL RIP YOUR STINKIN' EARS OFF!

361

GET IN HERE, **CREEP!**

B-BUT—YOU CAN'T ARREST HIM, JUDGE DREDD!

THE CREEP THREATENED TO RIP YOUR EARS OFF—DAMN RIGHT I'M ARRESTING HIM!

BUT YOUNG **SLASHER** WAS MERELY EXERCISING HIS **FREEDOM OF EXPRESSION.** THAT'S SOMETHING WE HERE AT REHAB TRY TO **ENCOURAGE!**

362

THIS JOB'S MAKIN' YOU SOFT IN THE HEAD, WILLIAMS! IT'S NO GOOD LETTING THESE LITTLE CREEPS WALK ALL OVER YOU. THEY NEED **DISCIPLINE!**

NOT AT ALL, JUDGE DREDD! QUITE THE REVERSE, IN FACT! OUR POLICY HERE AT REHAB IS TO TREAT THEM WITH TOLERANCE AND KINDNESS — A LITTLE TENDER, LOVING CARE.

AND IT **WORKS!**

WHY, WE HAVEN'T HAD A MAJOR VIOLENT INCIDENT HERE FOR, OH ... AT LEAST THREE DAYS!

363

SHATTER! ZIP ZIP ZIP ZIP

GEDDOWN!

SO MUCH FOR YOUR JUVES' GOOD CONDUCT MEDAL, COUNSELLOR!

WE'VE GOT A **RUMBLE** ON OUR HANDS!

364

THE— THE VIGILANTE!

N-NO! PLEASE! I— I NEVER DID NOTHIN' TO YOU!

THAT'S WHAT YOU THINK.

375

SO PERISH ALL SCUM!

THE BODIES OF THE VIGILANTE'S LATEST VICTIMS ARE DISCOVERED BY A PASSING CITIZEN AT 2105 HOURS—

THIS MUST BE MY LUCKY DAY! THANK YOU, BOYS!

IT IS ANOTHER HALF HOUR BEFORE MORE PUBLIC-SPIRITED CITIZENS CHANCE BY—

OH MY GRUD! CALL THE JUDGES!

376

THIS ONE LOOKS GENUINE, DREDD.

SIX VICTIMS, ALL MEMBERS OF THE GULAG JUVE GANG.

ALL BASED OUT OF THE ATLAS STREET JUVE REHAB— SAME AS THE VIGILANTE'S OTHER VICTIMS.

CAR WAS REPORTED STOLEN AN HOUR BACK.

ONE ODD THING—THEIR POCKETS HAVE BEEN CLEANED OUT, ALL CASH AND VALUABLES GONE.

IF IT IS THE VIGILANTE, LOOKS LIKE HE'S RUNNING SHORT OF FUNDS!

377

THAT BRINGS THE VIGILANTE'S TOTAL TO ELEVEN. WHOEVER HE IS, HE'S REALLY GOT IT IN FOR THOSE ATLAS STREET JUVES!

TROUBLE IS, EVERYBODY HATES THEM! WILLIAMS, THE REHAB COUNSELLOR, GAVE US A LONG LIST OF POSSIBLE SUSPECTS. WE CHECKED—ALL NEGATIVE!

WAIT A MINUTE... WILLIAMS!

378

WHAT IF IT'S NOT THE JUVES THE VIGILANTE'S GOT IT IN FOR? WHAT IF IT'S THEIR REHAB COUNSELLOR?

YOU MEAN, THE VIGILANTE IS KILLING WILLIAMS' JUVES TO GET AT HIM?

379

IT'S POSSIBLE. WORTH CHECKIN'. GET ONTO REHAB—SEE IF WILLIAMS HAS ANY KNOWN ENEMIES.

I'LL GO PAY HIM A PERSONAL!

AND IF YOU'RE JUST JOINING US— GOOD EVENING! I'M PETE PETRIE, AND HERE ARE THE RESULTS OF OUR LINE 9 VOTE IN!

SO FAR, OVER FOURTEEN THOUSAND VIDDERS HAVE CALLED IN TO VOTE. OF THOSE, A STARTLING 67 PERCENT ARE SOLIDLY BEHIND THE VIGILANTE'S ATTEMPTS TO EXTERMINATE THE CITY'S JUVE GANGS!

28 PERCENT SUPPORT SOME JUVE EXECUTIONS ... 4 PERCENT ARE TOTALLY OPPOSED TO THE VIGILANTE ... AND THE REMAINING ONE PERCENT CLAIMED TO ACTUALLY BE THE VIGILANTE!

JUDGE DREDD!

I'M HERE TO SEE WOLLISS WILLIAMS.

I'M AFRAID HE'S GONE OUT, JUDGE.

THEN MAYBE YOU CAN HELP!

381

YOU'VE HEARD OF THE VIGILANTE, CITIZEN WILLIAMS?

YES INDEED, JUDGE DREDD! HE'S THE ONE WHO'S BEEN KILLING ALL THE JUVES DOWN AT MY WOLLY'S REHAB!

THERE'S A POSSIBILITY THE VIGILANTE'S DOING IT TO GET AT YOUR SON ...

THEN HE'S GOING A FUNNY WAY ABOUT IT. AS FAR AS WOLLY'S CONCERNED, SCUM LIKE THEM ARE BETTER OFF DEAD!

382

LET ME GET THIS STRAIGHT, CITIZEN—YOUR SON DOESN'T LOVE HIS JUVES?

MERCY NO! WOLLY HATES THEIR GUTS!

OF COURSE, HE HAS TO PRETEND HE LIKES THEM. IT'S HIS JOB, YOU SEE— HE CAN'T AFFORD TO LOSE IT.

THAT SO?

383

SO ... THERE'S ANOTHER SIDE TO CITIZEN TENDER-LOVING-CARE WILLIAMS!

WHERE WAS YOUR SON LAST NIGHT — THE NIGHT BEFORE?

OUT. DOWN AT REHAB, I SUPPOSE.

WHAT ARE YOU SEARCHING FOR?

I'M NOT QUITE SURE ...

BUT THIS'LL DO!

DREDD TO CONTROL! I HAVE REASON TO BELIEVE REHAB COUNSELLOR *WOLLISS WILLIAMS* IS THE *VIGILANTE!*

MY WOLLY— THE VIGILANTE! HOW EXCITING!

ALL UNITS BE ON ALERT— VIGILANTE SUSPECT WOLLISS WILLIAMS, AGE 37, BROWN HAIR, SLIGHTLY BUILT, DRIVING BLACK FOORD MOOVER, REGISTRATION MBV/14/3MC!

ALL OVER THE CITY, JUDGES KEEP WATCH ...

WATCHING BAY 902 HERE! I SEE YOUR MAN!

NOW HEADING SOUTH DOWN ANDREW LLOYD BOULEVARD!

HE'S TURNING INTO BRIGHTMAN ROAD—MOVING OUT OF VISUAL!

BAY 903 HERE— I'VE GOT HIM!

386

WATCHING BAY 903! SUSPECT HAS PARKED, SIEVE STREET, NOW LEAVING VEHICLE.

SUSPECT IS MASKED—AND ARMED! OUR VIGILANTE ALL RIGHT!

MY DOK! THE BOP! HE'S GOING TO HIT THE JUVE BOP!

387

HE FELT CONFIDENT. ELEVEN JUVES HE'D KILLED, AND NO-ONE EVEN SUSPECTED HIM. AND THEY WOULDN'T— THEY NEVER WOULD.

AND HE KNEW WHY—BECAUSE WHAT HE WAS DOING WAS RIGHT AND JUST...

HEY—LOOK! IT'S ...

THE VIGILANTE— AAAARGH!

388

THE VIGILANTE! RUN!

AAAGH!

HE SQUEEZED THE TRIGGER. SQUEEZED AGAIN. EIGHT TIMES... NINE ... TEN ...

IN THE PANIC HE COULDN'T BE SURE OF HIS AIM. BUT WHAT DID IT MATTER? ALL JUVES WERE SCUM! ALL JUVES SHOULD DIE!

389

THE LAWMAN'S GUN BARKS ONCE —

AAH!

CONTROL! THE VIGILANTE IS DOWN. GET MED-SQUADS TO THE PALAIS DE BOP!

PICK UP YOUR GUN, COUNSELLOR.

YOU — YOU KNOW WHO I AM?

SURE ... MR TENDER-LOVING CARE! THE ONE PERSON WE NEVER THOUGHT TO CHECK

IT WAS A GOOD ACT, WILLIAMS — BUT I'M PULLING THE CURTAIN!

OKAY — SO I *AM* THE VIGILANTE! SO I HATE JUVES

BUT I'VE GOT GOOD REASON!

YOU DON'T KNOW WHAT IT WAS LIKE IN THAT REHAB — DAY AFTER DAY PUTTING UP WITH THE *ABUSE* — THE *INSULTS* — THE *VIOLENCE!* AND HAVING TO *SMILE* THROUGH IT ALL BECAUSE IF I DIDN'T, I'D LOSE MY JOB!

I GOT BAD NEWS FOR YOU, CREEP. YOU'VE *LOST* IT!

PICK UP YOUR GUN, VIGILANTE.

WH-WHY?

BECAUSE AT THE LAST COUNT THERE WERE OVER 100 JUVES DEAD IN *COPYCAT MURDERS* — AND EVERY ONE OF THEM IS DOWN TO YOU!

FOR THE GOOD OF THE CITIZENRY, I'M GOING TO HAVE TO MAKE AN *EXAMPLE.*

YOU — YOU CAN'T MAKE ME DO THIS, JUDGE DREDD! I DON'T HAVE A CHANCE!

A BETTER CHANCE THAN YOU GAVE THE JUVES YOU SLAUGHTERED.

YOU STARTED THIS GAME, WILLIAMS — I'M GOING TO MAKE SURE YOU SEE IT THROUGH. NOW *PICK UP THE GUN!*

END OF STORY

"PICKED UP FOR LOITERING, AGE SEVEN. NOW AGE SIXTEEN. MOTHER DECEASED, LIVES WITH FATHER. PRETTY WELL OFF — FATHER OWNS *HARCOURT HOLDINGS.* THAT'S A TURNOVER OF OVER *90 MILLION* LAST YEAR."

"TRY THE NUMBER."

BREEE

BREEE BREEE BREEE..

BREEE BREEE

DREDD?

NO, IT'S SANTA CLAUS.

WE'VE GOT DAVID HARCOURT. YOU WANT TO SEE HIM ALIVE AGAIN, YOU'LL HAVE TO **PAY** FOR THE PRIVILEGE.

LOOKS LIKE HIS **FATHER** ALREADY **DID.**

THAT WAS AN **ACCIDENT.** WE DIDN'T KNOW HE'D BE THERE.

TOO BAD, BECAUSE YOU JUST KILLED YOUR GOLDEN GOOSE. ME, I DON'T MAKE DEALS.

YOU'D **BETTER.** LISTEN...

AAAHH! NO — STOP!

PERP'S USING SOME KIND OF **MUFFLER** ON HIS VOICE...

BUT THAT'S THE BOY ALL RIGHT. WE'VE CHECKED IT AGAINST RECORDINGS IN THE APARTMENT.

HELP ME... PLEASE..!

YOU WILL BE CONTACTED.

SECURITY CAMERA TOOK THIS. NEIGHBOURS SAY THERE WAS A THIRD MAN, WAITING OUT-SIDE IN A BLACK ROADSTER, PROBABLY STOLEN. WE'VE GOT AN **APB** OUT.

ANYONE GIVE A DESCRIPTION OF THE MEN?

NOTHING GOOD ENOUGH TO GO ON.

THE GRAND HALL OF JUSTICE.

DAVID WAS A SHY BOY... UNCOMMUNICATIVE. INTROVERTED, YOU'D HAVE TO SAY.

OF COURSE, HECK WAS TO BLAME. HECK, THAT'S HIS FATHER...

DAVID NEVER QUITE LIVED UP TO HIS EXPECTATIONS. WHATEVER DAVID DID, IT WASN'T ENOUGH. IT DROVE THE BOY INTO HIS SHELL...

YOUR NEPHEW HAVE ANY CLOSE FRIENDS, MRS PHEWS?

NO...HE DIDN'T MAKE FRIENDS EASILY. HE PLAYED ROLE GAMES A LOT, BUT I DON'T THINK HE MADE ANY REAL FRIENDS THERE.

ROLE GAMES... PEOPLE WHO FEEL OUT OF TUNE WITH THE REAL WORLD OFTEN TURN TO FANTASY...

BLEEE

LABS. WE'VE GOT SOMETHING — CAN YOU COME DOWN?

CHECK.

POOR DAVID — HE WAS QUITE A NICE BOY UNDERNEATH...

IS, MRS PHEWS. AS FAR AS WE KNOW, YOUR NEPHEW IS STILL ALIVE.

I'M SORRY...

WE'VE GOT DAVID HARCOURT. YOU WANT TO SEE HIM ALIVE AGAIN, YOU'LL HAVE TO PAY FOR THE PRIVILEGE.

NOW LET'S JUST DAMP DOWN THE VOICE AND BRING UP THE BACKGROUND NOISE...

We've got David Harcourt. You want to see him alive again. You'll have to

The 23·20 Zoom to Lambert Hall is running seven minutes late. We apologise for

BINGO!

44

"THE 23·20 WAS DELAYED FOR ANOTHER ELEVEN MINUTES AT PASKIE. THERE'S ONLY **ONE** STATION THE ANNOUNCEMENT COULD'VE BEEN MADE..."

"...CLEVELAND STREET."

CONTROL ! I WANT ANY UNITS YOU CAN SPARE TO ASSIST IN SEARCH, CLEVELAND STREET AREA !

KID HAD A THING ABOUT FANTASY GAMES. I WONDER...

LOCKED...

FANTASY REALMS

GEEZ! HOW'D HE *FIND* US?

WHAT'RE WE GONNA *DO*, RANCIE?

BLOOD...

LOOKS LIKE I'VE COME TO THE RIGHT PLACE...

WE GOTTA MAKE SURE HE NEVER LEAVES HERE ALIVE!

COME ON!

CHANGG!

I AM THE DUNGEON MASTER!

YOUR QUEST HAS BEGUN! WILL YOU FIND THE UNIMAGINED TREASURES YOU SEEK—OR ONLY TERROR AND OBLIVION? THE ANSWER LIES IN YOUR HANDS ALONE!

LASER IMAGE!

THREE DOORS LIE OPEN TO YOU. CHOOSE ONE— AND MAY GOOD FORTUNE GO WITH YOU...

...OR **NOT**, AS THE CASE MAY BE! HAHAHAHAHA-HAHAHAHA!

THE IMAGINE VANISHES...

OKAY, LET'S JUST PLAY ALONG, SEE WHERE IT LEADS...

MORE PASSAGES ACROSS THE CHASM...

WHO COMES CLIP-CLIP-CLOPPING ACROSS **MY** BRIDGE?

THAT'S GOT TO BE A ROBOT!

GIVE ME ONE REASON I SHOULDN'T **GOBBLE YOU UP** HERE AND NOW, WORM!

HOW ABOUT A HIGH EXPLOSIVE BULLET?

BADOM!

ZINGG!

I HAVEN'T GOT TIME TO MESS WITH YOU, PAL! MOVE, OR YOU'RE AN *EX-TROLL!*

THEN DIE!

KRA-CHAK!

SPLA-KISSHH!

'FRAID IT'S THE SAME ANSWER—

—HIGH EX!

DON'T TELL ME— GIVE YOU ONE REASON WHY YOU SHOULDN'T GOBBLE ME UP NOW, HUH?

SOMEONE FIRING! CRACK IN THE WALL UP THERE..!

VDANNGG!

RICOCHET!

AAGGK!

AAAHH!

VDANNGGG!

VDANNGG!

51

THEY LIKE TO PLAY IT **ROUGH** IN THIS PLACE! BETTER MARK IT DOWN FOR A COMPLETE **SAFETY CHECK.**

RANCIE..!

PROBABLY SOME SORT OF **MAINTENANCE TUNNEL** UP THERE...

...AND I KNOW JUST HOW TO **REACH** IT!

IF I CAN JUST LASSO THAT ROCK, I— BINGO!

THESE PASSAGES PROBABLY RUN ALL *AROUND* DUNGEON REALM...

WHICH WAY NOW?

IT'S *DREDD!* HE'S FOUND US!

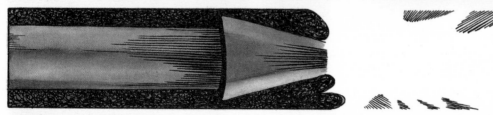

P-CHOWW!

AARRHH!

NO—!

EEEUUGHH!

KLUNNG!

YES... DEFINITELY GOING TO HAVE TO RUN A SAFETY CHECK ON THIS PLACE..!

YOU'LL BE ALL RIGHT NOW, SON...AT LEAST, AS RIGHT AS YOU CAN *EVER* BE AFTER THIS.

TWO OF THE MEN WERE *DUNGEON MASTERS*, EMPLOYED BY *FANTASTIC VOYAGE*. THEY MUST'VE RECOGNISED DAVID HARCOURT AND SEEN AN OPPORTUNITY TO TURN THEIR *OWN* FANTASIES INTO REALITY.

JUST ONE BIG ROLE-PLAYING GAME — ONLY THIS TIME THE STAKES WERE *LIFE AND DEATH*...

TOO BAD FOR THEM THEY RAN INTO THE *REAL* DUNGEON MASTER!

Arthur Ranson

REAL NAME: ARTHUR RANSON
SOCIAL CATEGORY: ARTIST
STATUS: ACTIVE
CURRENT PROJECT: JUDGE ANDERSON

FAVOURITE FILMS

1   The Seven Samurai
2   Blade Runner
3   Breaking Away
4   The Silence
5   Viva Zapata
6   Pinocchio
7   The Navigator
8   The Naked Prey
9   The Adventures Of Robin Hood (1939)
10   The Manchurian Candidate

FAVOURITE TV SHOWS

1   The Singing Detective
2   Game Set And Match
3   Bugs Bunny/Daffy Duck
4   The Insurance Man (play)
5   M.A.S.H.
6   Victoria Wood
7   Red Dwarf
8   Horizon
9   Newsnight
10   Hancock's Half Hour

FAVOURITE RECORDS

1   Verdi: Requiem
2   Lyons After-Dinner Classics
3   Ringo Starr: Goodnight Vienna
4   Rubenstein Plays Chopin Waltzes
5   Berlin Philharmoniker: Adagio
6   Phil Spector: Greatest Hits
7   Beethoven: The Complete Works
8   The Singing Detective (Compilation)
9   Enrique Bátiz: French Orchestral Masterpieces
10   Bruce Springsteen: Born To Run

FAVOURITE COMICS

1   The Airtight Garage (Moebius)
2   Watchmen
3   Conan (Thamas/Buscema Version)
4   Tarzan Of The Apes (Hogarth)
5   Dark Knight
6   Lone Sloane
7   Asterix
8   The Adventures Of Luther Arkwright
9   Lady Chatterley's Lover (Emerson)
10   Exterminateur 17

FAVOURITE BOOKS

1   The Chronicles Of Thomas Covenant: Stephen Donaldson
2   Children Of Violence: Doris Lessing
3   Ulysses: James Joyce
4   Tarzan Of The Apes: Edgar Rice Burroughs
5   The Atlantic Book Of British & American Poetry
6   Joseph And His Brothers: Thomas Mann
7   The 'Rabbit' Series: John Updike
8   The Brothers Karamazov: Dostoyevsky
9   The Glass Bead Game: Herman Hesse
10   Lake Wobegon Days: Garrison Keillor

REAL NAME: ALAN DAVIS
SOCIAL CATEGORY: ARTIST
STATUS: ACTIVE
CURRENT PROJECT: EXCALIBUR

FAVOURITE FILMS

1. Animal House
2. Some Like It Hot
3. The Odd Couple
4. The Long Goodbye
5. It's A Wonderful Life
6. Arsenic And Old Lace
7. A Matter Of Life And Death
8. The Sweet Smell Of Success
9. El Dorado
10. Educating Rita

FAVOURITE TV SHOWS

1. Auf Wiedersehen Pet
2. Sherlock Holmes (Jeremy Brett)
3. Paperchase
4. Rich Man Poor Man
5. The Rockford Files
6. Callan
7. Boys From The Blackstuff
8. Fawlty Towers
9. Star Trek
10. Lou Grant

FAVOURITE RECORDS

1. Elton John: Goodbye Yellow Brick Road
2. Elton John: Caribou
3. Elton John: Captain Fantastic
4. Dionne Warwick Sings Bacharach
5. Elkie Brooks: The Very Best Of
6. Squeeze: Argybargy
7. Don McLean: American Pie
8. George Gershwin: Gershwin Classics
9. Nat King Cole: Unforgettable
10. Madness: Complete Madness

FAVOURITE COMICS

1. X-Men 56-65
2. Garth (Daily Mirror)
3. Red Nails M.T.E.4
4. Green Lantern Corp Annual 1
5. Swamp Thing 12
6. Mister Miracle 24-25
7. Lance McLean (Daily Record)
8. Silver Surfer 4
9. Dan Dare: The Man From Nowhere
10. New Mutants 21

FAVOURITE BOOKS

1. Mars Series: Edgar Rice Burroughs
2. Lensman Series: E.E. Doc Smith
3. Conan: Robert E. Howard
4. Wuthering Heights: Emily Brontë
5. Last Of The Mohicans: James Fenimore Cooper
6. Gullivar's Travels (5) Dean Jonathon Swift
7. The Ragged Trousered Philanthropist: Robert (Noonan) Trestle
8. The Time Machine: H.G. Wells
9. She: H. Rider Haggard
10. A Christmas Carol: Charles Dickens

IT'S A MAD, mad, M9D WORLD!

HOW LONG HAD IT BEEN GOING ON? THIS CRAZY WAR... FIGHT AND KILL, FIGHT AND KILL...

SCRIPT
MIKE COLLINS
ART
ALAN DAVIS
LETTERING
GLOP

FIGHT AND—

—KILL.

BZAK
K

THEY KEEP COMING... I KEEP KILLING.

BUT I'M NOT A WARRIOR. I DON'T EVEN BELONG ON THIS ALIEN HELLHOLE. I'M AN EARTHMAN...

...I WAS ONE OF FIFTY EMISSARIES SENT FROM EARTH ON THE SPACESHIP EXCALIBUR, IN RESPONSE TO MAN'S FIRST CONTACT WITH AN ALIEN RACE.

THE MESSAGE HAD ORIGINATED FROM THE PLANET *ELYSIUS,* PROMISING FRIENDSHIP AND THE EXCHANGE OF KNOWLEDGE.

YET, WHEN WE ARRIVED, THE WORLD SEEMED DESERTED. WE FOUND NONE OF THE EXPECTED SIGNS OF LIFE, UNTIL —

CAPTAIN, WE'RE PICKING UP SOMETHING NOW, SIR. MUST BE A *CITY,* STRONG *POLLUTION* AND *BACKGROUND RADIATION* READINGS.

TAKE US IN THEN. LET'S GET THIS *WELCOME* WE WERE PROMISED!

CAPTAIN! *MALFUNCTION!* THE SHIP'S GONE OUT OF CONTROL! WE'RE GOING TO —

KRKOOOM

THE *EXCALIBUR* WAS TOTALLY DESTROYED. ALL THE EMISSARIES WERE KILLED. THE CAPTAIN, JEAN AND I SURVIVED ONLY BECAUSE THE SHIP'S BRIDGE HAD BEEN EJECTED ON IMPACT.

WHAT HAPPENS NOW? WE'VE NO FOOD AND NO CONTACT WITH EARTH...

MAYBE WE CAN GET SOME HELP FROM THE ALIENS —

THEIR KIND OF HELP WE CAN DO WITHOUT! LOOK AT THIS *LASER HIT!* THEY *SHOT US DOWN!* THE MESSAGE LIED! THESE PEOPLE ARE VIOLEN...

LOOK OUT!

AARGH!

SHNNT

GRZAK

RRRK!!

CAPTAIN!

HE'S DEAD, WE CAN'T HELP HIM!

WE'VE GOT TO GET TO COVER— GET AWAY!

BUT THEY'RE TAKING HIS BODY!

THIS IS NO TIME FOR SENTIMENT— JUST RUN!

FOR HOURS WE RAN, THROUGH A BLASTED ALIEN LANDSCAPE OF WAR-TORN INSANITY, UNTIL...

CAN'T RUN ANYMORE... FEELING SICK... WHATEVER WAS ON THAT SPEAR...

KEEP CONTROL—THE STERA-PATCH BANDAGE SHOULD TAKE CARE OF ANY INFECTION...

KRSSSH

MORE ALIENS!

RELAX, THEY'RE TOO BUSY KILLING EACH OTHER TO NOTICE US.

THIS IS INSANE... CONSTANT DEATH AND DESTRUCTION... WE BELIEVED IN THE MESSAGE THEY SENT... THEY PROMISED PEACE... FRIENDSHIP...

WE MOVED ON, TAKING FALLEN WEAPONS TO DEFEND OURSELVES WITH...

...QUICKLY LEARNING HOW TO USE THEM...HOW TO FIGHT...HOW TO KILL...

FIGHTING, KILLING, BOTH BECAME A REFLEX ACTION—

RICK... I FEEL ILL...

RICK... RRR...

RKKKKKKKKKK...

J-JEAN?

HER WOUND...THE INFECTION HAD SOMEHOW MUTATED HER...

I KILLED HER...WITHOUT THINKING, JUST LIKE ALL THE OTHERS...

BAM BAM BDAM

NOW I'M ALONE...

ALONE ON THIS CRAZY WARWORLD...

...SO I FIGHT.

AND THE LONGER I STAY HERE, THE MORE LIKE THEM I BECOME...

IT'S IRONIC THAT MAN'S FIRST CONTACT IS WITH A RACE MORE WARLIKE THAN HIMSELF...

CAN ONLY HOPE THAT I'M THE LAST EARTHMAN TO SEE THIS HELLHOLE...

...AND THAT EARTH SENDS NO MORE MISSIONS TO THIS INSANE WORLD...

THARG TRANSLATION:
DANGER
PSYCHOTIC JUVENILES' CONTAINMENT FACILITY

Now on Sale at a Thrill Merchant near You!

Published by Fleetway Publications, Greater London House, Hampstead Road, London NW1 7QQ, a member of Maxwell Magazine Publishing Corporation Ltd. Sole Agents: Australia and New Zealand, Gordon & Gotch Ltd., South Africa, Central News Agency Ltd. All rights reserved and reproduction without permission strictly forbidden. Printed by Rotolitho Lombarda, Italy. Reproduction by Melbourne Graphics, London. © Fleetway Publications, 1989.

GOOD. THESE PROBLEMS AREN'T UNCOMMON. **ALL** JUDGES GO THROUGH THEM SOONER OR LATER.

I WANT TO DELVE INTO YOUR **PAST**. SEE IF I CAN GET AT THE **ROOT** OF THE TROUBLE.

THIS INJECTION WILL HELP OVERCOME YOUR RESISTANCE TO **HYPNOSIS**.

RELAX. FOCUS ON THE **STROBE**. LET YOUR CONSCIOUS MIND **SLIP AWAY**.

I WANT TO TAKE YOU **BACK**...

BACK...

BACK...

BACK...

CASETAPE: DREDD SEG 01

YOU ARE **FIVE** YEARS OLD—

FIVE...

—YOU HAVE JUST ENTERED THE **ACADEMY OF LAW**. HOW DO YOU FEEL?

STRANGE...I'M WITH OTHERS, BUT I FEEL ALONE. . . CONFUSED...

DREDD'S THOUGHT WAVES ARE TRANSLATED INTO VISUAL IMAGES ON RHEINHART'S MONITOR—

WHAT AM I DOING HERE? WHO **AM** I?

DON'T YOU KNOW?

YOU'VE JUST SHOT **RICO.** DOES IT... DISTURB YOU?

NATURALLY. HE **IS** MY CLONE-BROTHER.

SO YOU'VE NEVER OVERCOME YOUR FEELINGS FOR HIM?

NO. BUT IT DIDN'T STOP ME DOING MY DUTY.

LET'S TALK ABOUT THESE **DOUBTS** YOU'VE BEEN HAVING. THE **BUNT** CASE, FOR INSTANCE – YOU CLAIM YOU DIDN'T HAVE TO KILL THIS PERP?

NO, I COULD HAVE DISARMED HIM.

BUT THE **KILL** SHOT IS **STANDARD PROCEDURE.**

I MEAN, THIS CREEP'S JUST GUTTED AN OLD-AGE CIT – GRUD KNOWS HOW MANY OTHERS BEFORE YOU CAUGHT HIM.

WHAT DO YOU WANT TO DO, PAT HIM ON THE BUTT AND SAY "DON'T DO IT AGAIN"?

RELEASE WAS NOT AN OPTION. YOU'RE **DISTORTING** THE ISSUE, RHEINHART.

"THEN THERE'S THE **CRICKLE** GIRL."

"YES. I KNOW NOW, I SHOULD NEVER HAVE GOT INVOLVED."

"BUT YOU DID. **WHY** ?"

"I DON'T KNOW, RHEINHART. **YOU'RE** THE SHRINK — YOU TELL **ME**."

AFTER THE EXAMINATION — "THERE'S NOTHING IN HIS HISTORY I CAN PINPOINT AS THE CAUSE OF THESE LAPSES. JUST THE NORMAL REACTION TO PROLONGED CONTACT WITH THE CITIZENRY, I'M AFRAID.

NO MATTER HOW HARD WE TRY TO CONTROL IT, SOONER OR LATER THE HUMAN BEING BEHIND THE MASK ALWAYS STARTS TO COME OUT, EVEN IN A STREET-HARD JUDGE LIKE DREDD."

"SO WHAT DO WE DO ABOUT IT ?"

"IF HE KEEPS BROODING HE MAY BEGIN TO QUESTION HIS ROLE — HIS VERY FUNCTION AS A JUDGE. WE COULD **LOSE** HIM."

"THAT'S UNACCEPTABLE!"

"THEN I'D RECOMMEND IMMEDIATE **PSYCHO-SURGERY**. WE'LL BURN OUT THE EMBRYONIC EMOTIONAL CENTRES."

"NO!"

"SURGERY WOULD **DIMINISH** THE MAN. IF DREDD HAS PROBLEMS HE MUST OVERCOME THEM BY HIS OWN STRENGTH OF CHARACTER — HIS OWN WILL. THAT'S WHAT MAKES HIM THE JUDGE HE IS.

IN THAT CASE, KEEP HIM BUSY. DON'T GIVE HIM TIME TO BROOD. GET HIM AWAY FROM HIS **USUAL ROUTINE** BY ALL MEANS — BUT KEEP HIM BUSY."

"VERY WELL. HE'S GOT A SMALL CASE OF ARMS DEALING TO CLEAR UP; THEN I HAVE JUST THE MISSION FOR HIM...

IT WILL BE HIS STERNEST TEST SINCE THE APOCALYPSE WAR !"

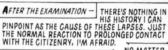

CONTINUED
● **ON PAGE 75** ●

THE MEGA-CITY SPORT

Mega-City One's CRUSADING Newspaper

Wednesday August 20, 2112　　10cr

WORLD EXCLUSIVE PICTURES STUN SCIENTISTS!

PHOTO: JEFF ANDERSON

JUSTICE DEPT H-WAGON FOUND ON **Intergalactic EXCLUSIVE** MOON!

MUTANT HELL OF SEXY TELLY STAR
SEE BACK PAGE!

by Jack Hack, Space Correspondent

CHIEF JUDGE tells Justice Dept to tow home lost craft.

FIVE top space-trained judges have blasted off from Mega-City One Space Port on a top secret mission to recover a vintage Justice Dept H-Wagon found on the Moon.

Headed by Senior Judge Dredd, the Justice Dept team took off on a classified mission earlier this week.

But the news blackout is shattered today by these amazing satellite pictures of the H-Wagon where it was found 238,885 miles from home.

No wonder it was a classified mission.

"The Justice Dept obviously wants to bring back the H-Wagon without anyone knowing," confirmed space boffin Dr Hugo Hackenbush.

The ricketty old H-Wagon mysteriously VANISHED in July after the Sunday Meg stunned scientists with pictures of it in orbit around the Earth.

The Justice Dept admits that a specialist in these early H-Wagons, Judge "Mitch" Mitch, is aboard the moon shuttle.

"This H-Wagon could be the key to cheap space travel," said a Justice Dept financial spokesperson. "We want to know how that old crate got to the moon on only one tank of fuel."

*FULL STORY PAGE 13

71

HOOD LUM!

A ROBIN HOOD-STYLE maniac fired arrows at Judges as they tried to arrest him, it was revealed yesterday.

A worried band of Judges had to don full riot gear as they came under a hail of deadly missiles at the Salvation Army Centre on Booth Boulevard.

A local Sector House spokesman said, "This unfortunate man appears to be under the delusion that he is the reincarnation of Michael Praed. Nothing ten years in the Cubes won't cure."

WORLD EXCLUSIVE PICTURES STUN SCIENTISTS!

AN ARROWING EXPERIENCE — ten years for this per

NICE ONE, SQUIRREL

PHOTO: JEFF ANDERSON

WORLD EXCLUSIVE PICTURES STUN SCIENTISTS!

GREAT BALLS OF FUR — it's enough to drive you nuts

VETERAN golfer Mahatma Kane Jeeves thought he'd heard every hard luck story – until a squirrel picked his ball off the Fairway at the Mega-City One Municipal Golf Club. The Mahatma, a spry 67, had just driven off from the Club's first and only tee when the squirrel jumped from the tree, tucked the ball under its arm and disappeared. Said the Mahatma, "I am being very upset. I have been on a waiting list for seven years for this game, and now I haven't the balls to play. Dearie, dearie." He lost by default.

PLENTY OF GUM-PTION

SNEAK THIEF Vincenz Alcazam's victims were gob struck. Because all he eve nicked were their gnashers When Judges finally tracked hir down and searched hi apartment, they found 40 sets c false teeth being used a doorstops, toe-nail clippers, pie crust trimmers, hairbrushes an drawer handles. Now the owner face a king-size headache sorting out which teeth belong t whom.

LUBBER SOUL

HONDO-CIT scientists have come up with the ultimate in rubber gloves. As soon as you dip your hands in the washing up water, they begin to sing the classic Beatles number, "Love me do." Why?

UGLY BUG GRAN HAS BRAIN CUT OUT

by Wolf J. Flywheel

Horror Op to Re-Site Monster Eyeballs

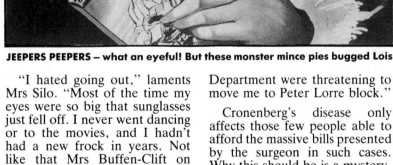

JEEPERS PEEPERS – what an eyeful! But these monster mince pies bugged Lois

FRANKENSTEIN docs scooped out a goggle-eyed gran's brain to cure her eyesight.

Surgeons performed the horror-op on Mrs Lois Silo after a rare disease turned her into a bug-eyed monster.

For the bubbly 48 year-old could not venture outside without passers-by staring at the grotesque bulging eyes protruding from her face.

"My right eye stuck out further than my left. It was gross. It was so big, it even began to hang over my lower eyelid. The pictures stunned scientists." Lois had been suffering from Cronenberg's Disease – a rare disorder in which the body begins to spontaneously deform. There is only one known cure, an operation in which the head is cut from ear to ear and the brain lifted out, so that surgeons can relieve pressure on the eyeballs from the inside.

"I hated going out," laments Mrs Silo. "Most of the time my eyes were so big that sunglasses just fell off. I never went dancing or to the movies, and I hadn't had a new frock in years. Not like that Mrs Buffen-Clift on level two. Some people just throw their creds away on the most *declassé* concoctions from that grave-robber down at Emilio's Dress Emporium. Anyway, where was I? Oh yes, I was a prisoner in my own home for four years."

The former librarian and winner of the Regional Medal for Good Citizenship – she informed on over fourteen of her grandchildren – had suffered constant pain for nearly six years when she opted for the dangerous, eight-hour eye-positioning operation.

Said Lois, "I didn't care about the risks, I had to have the operation. The Justice Department were threatening to move me to Peter Lorre block."

Cronenberg's disease only affects those few people able to afford the massive bills presented by the surgeon in such cases. Why this should be is a mystery, even to accountants.

"To complete successful surgery you have to reposition the eyeballs by going in through the skull and lifting out the brain", said Doctor Bing Pretorious, the surgeon in charge. "Ensuring that you replace all of the brain is crucial. If even a tiny piece is left out, patients have been known to become resentful and abusive, even violent. Some refuse to pay the bill at all, and threaten to damage the surgeon's own brain tissue. We offer a counselling service for such unfortunates in Mike Tyson block," he added helpfully.

73

ACTRESS FIGHTS OFF ALIEN PEEPING TOM

PHOTO: JEFF ANDERSON

WORLD EXCLUSIVE PICTURES STUN SCIENTISTS!

WATCH THIS SPACE – but intergalactic ogling was one close encounter too many for saucy Suz

AWARD-WINNING actress Suzy Q last night told how she was spied upon by a peeping tom alien.

When the star prepared for bed she didn't realise that she was the star of a private show. An alien was peering in her window – forty floors up!

"I was undressing for bed and looking out of the window and I could see lots of

SICK SPACEMAN

tiny red and green lights drifting around outside the window," said Suzy, vid star and queen of the political gossip columns.

When the astonished fifty on year-old actress dashed t investigate she found that th little blue men had scarpere back to their saucer.

The warped-out spac travellers then tried to use a invisible beam to drag the sta into the saucer.

"I had to use every ounc of will to keep my feet on th floor," she recalled.

PERPIE
by Worthington J. Kinklemellow III

GEE, JUDGE! YOU'RE SO HANDSOME, TALL AND STRONG!

YOU'RE DOING TIME, CREEP!

SAY, JUDGE! THERE'S A LITTLE PROBLEM OVER AT SAM FOX BLOCK WHERE I LIVE! COULD YOU COME OVER AND SORT IT OUT?

LIE DETECTOR SAYS YOU'RE NOT TELLING THE TRUTH, CITIZEN! FLIRTING WITH A JUDGE IS ALSO AN OFFENCE...

...30 DAYS IN AN ISO-CUBE FOR YOU!

WHOOPS! LOOKS LIKE I'VE BEEN BUSTED AGAIN!

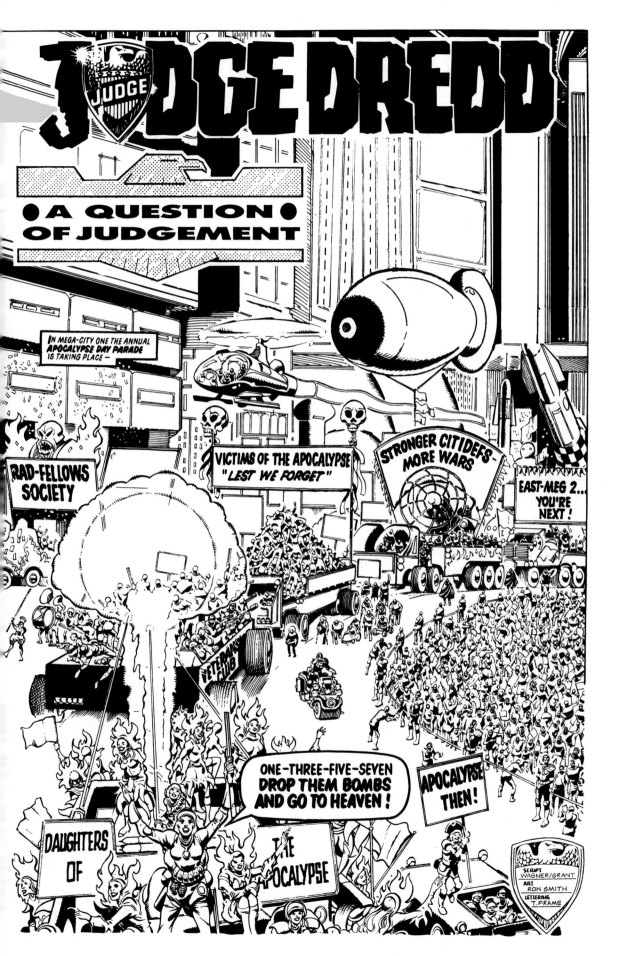

IT HAPPENED YESTERDAY. I'VE BEEN THINKING ABOUT IT EVER SINCE.

IT WAS A RUN OF THE MILL **ARV** TURNED HOMICIDE.

PERP NAME OF **FESTER BUNT**...

STOP!

DROP YOUR WEAPON!

DROP **DEAD**, LAWMAN!

B LAM!

BADAM!

AAAGH!

SURE, THAT'S ONE WAY. SOME TAKE A DESK JOB FOR A WHILE – SOME GO SEE THE SHRINK. TELL YOU HOW I GOT OVER IT.

TIGHT BOOTS.

ONE MORE SHOVE IN THE BACK, SONNY, AN' I'LL HAVE YOU IN THE JUVE CUBES BEFORE YOUR STREET CREEPERS TOUCH THE GROUND!

ULP!

TIGHT BOOTS?

SURE. SEE, ALL I NEEDED WAS SOMETHING TO TAKE MY MIND OFF THINGS, STOP ME BROODING. SO I CHANGED MY BOOTS – STARTED WEARING A SIZE TOO SMALL.

BY GRUD, DID THOSE BOOTS HURT!

THING IS, JOE, I SPENT SO MUCH TIME CURSING OUT THOSE DAMNED BOOTS, I FORGOT ALL ABOUT MY OTHER WORRIES. I'VE NEVER LOOKED BACK SINCE.

ALL RIGHT, CLOWN! I WARNED YOU!

IT-IT WASN'T ME, SIR! IT'S THEM BEHIND ME PUSHIN'!

THANKS FOR THE ADVICE, MORPH.

SURE, JOE. AND REMEMBER, WHEN IT COMES DOWN TO THE BOTTOM LINE, THAT CREEP'S GOT NO COMPLAINT.

HE KNEW THE RULES. HE SACRIFICED HIS RIGHT TO LIVE AS SOON AS HE TURNED THAT GUN ON A JUDGE.

MORPH!

ALL RIGHT! THAT'S IT! **YOU** AN' **YOU** AN' **YOU**! I'M HANDIN' OUT **TIME** NOW!

LATER—

TIGHT BOOTS, HUH? THAT'S A GOOD ONE!

STORES

HMMM.

STILL...

...YOU NEVER KNOW.

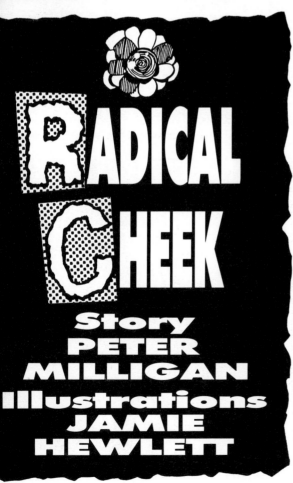

RADICAL CHEEK

Story PETER MILLIGAN

Illustrations JAMIE HEWLETT

Okay, Max,' snarled Judge Dredd, grabbing me roughly by the umbrella. 'I'm pulling you and all the Normals in.'

'Hey, Dreddio!' I said. 'Don't blow my zeal with that zany spiel. This is my big day! This is the day of the Max Normal Mega-City Fashion Show! Rest the jest, Man. I mean, take a dive with that jive and let a cool cat stay alive!'

Hey, listen. Maybe I should start at the beginning. That's the *normal* thing to do, is it not? I'm Max Normal. I'm the King of Kool, the chap with the rap, and I'd arrived at one of my MAX NORMAL BOUTIQUES only to see that Dredd and some of the other Judges were already there. All my staff and a flare of Normal shoppers were either lined up against a wall or being thrown into Crim-Wagons. Was this a nightmare or was this a nightmare? Later that day I was going to have my biggest fashion bash yet, the Max Normal Mega-City Fashion Show, featuring a new line of thirty-inch flared pin-striped suits, with matching handkerchiefs and bowler hats, all the fab gear it takes to make a Norm top of the form, and here was Dredd laying down some krazy karma, saying how he was going to throw my hide inside a Crim-Cube. Get ye behind me, mindblower! ▶

'For old times sake, Dredd baby,' I said. 'Give m
the rundown on what's come down. Give Max th
facts.'

As you know, old Dredd has got a soft spot fo
Maxie. It's a soft spot about two inches below th
solar plexus, and this is where he hit me, with hi
elbow.

'Not this time, Normal. Your followers are
public menace.'

I hit the ground. But I hit it with style. the
don't call me the Sheik of Chic for nothing. The
wouldn't call me the Sultan of *Soigné* if I couldn'
take a little blow down below.

'Freeze out, Daddy. Just give me a sign c
what's out of line. Maybe I can give the long arr
of the law a hand!'

Dredd pulled me to my feet and dragged m
away from the boutique, then he threw m
against a wall and pushed his face so close t
mine I could see my reflection in his visor. M
reflection looked as good as ever. It's nice t
know you can still count on *some* things.

'Okay, Normal,' grunted Dredd, without movin
his lips. 'I'll give you one chance. Overnight ther
has been an outbreak of criminal activity by Ma
Normal fashion followers. Bank jobs, mugging:
vandalism; you name it, those punks have don
it. All the normalite punks are wearing you
clothes, Normal. They're your followers. If yo
don't clear it up in five hours, I'm closing dow
your boutiques and making the possession c
flared trousers a criminal offence.'

With that, Dredd elbowed me once more fc
luck in that soft spot beneath my solar plexu
and sped off on his bike. If it weren't for his dres
sense, that Judge would have a mile of style.

So this was the score with the law. Som
renegade Normals were causing a sti
and if I didn't want to end up in st
myself I had to get to the bottom of
and come out on top. The future of flare
trousers rested in my hands. I had five hours t
stop my cool crown slipping. I had five hours t
save the Max Normal Mega City Fashion Show.
knew, in the name of everything pin-striped, tha
I couldn't afford to lose.

So I lost no time in going round the boutique
and fashion stores. I flashed the cash, I didn
stifle the rifle, I laid the creds on all the heads i
the know, trying to clue in on any new blood tha
was buying the Normal line of menswear.

Now, one thing you chucks and chicks shoul
know about the fashion world is that it's a jungle
It's full of gangsters, crooks, protection racket
pay-offs, lay-offs, day-offs and corruption.

ther words, the fashion game is the same as
everything else in Mega-City One.

And while I looked for a clue as to what was
ew I kept asking myself a question or two: why
hould there suddenly be an outbreak of lawless-
ess by cats in bowler hats? By guys in striped
es? By dregs in flared pegs?

I had no luck with the normal cats and
kitties. No one knew a thing. No-one
could tell why dedicated followers of
Max Normal had suddenly turned into
razy lawbreaking dudes.

I decided to visit the high guru of the mean
ashion scene: Old Man Ross. The old man is
razier than a three-eyed cyclops, and you can't
ust chat cat to cat with him: he insists on
utting you in front of an old camera and
nterviewing you. But I was running out of ideas
nd running out of time. If I didn't get a lead soon
d lose my fashion show, and the world would be
entenced to a fate worse than drainpipe
rousers.

Old Man Ross spent about three minutes asking
e about my life and my stranger habits, and
hen I managed to throw him a question.

'Hey, Man. Can you give me a rundown on what
appened at sundown? Last night scores of
oots wearing my suits started to loot, and
therwise rave to a crime wave.'

'Sowwy, Max. Can't help. But if you'd like to lie
own I'll show you how to leg westle. It's weally
un. . .'

Poor old Ross. One of these days the only
erson he'll have left to interview is himself. I left
im lying on his back waving his legs in the air
nd went outside to resume my search. Three
ours had passed, and I still hadn't a clue as to
hat made my fashion followers turn criminal. I
ecided to try the low end of the market, the
rubby clothes stalls frequented by the kitsch
nd fameless.

Fifteen minutes later I was strolling through
he shabby makeshift stalls of the shabby
akeshift garment district of Mega-City.
aturally, I was attracting some attention.
ormalites were gathering around me, begging
e for fashion tips. How pencil thin should pencil
hin moustaches be? Should bowler hats be
pped to the left or the right? You know the sort
f thing. One finely dressed young cat came up
o me, and asked if I would autograph his sock
uspender.

'I see you're wearing one of my Leon Brittan
hunky Pin Stripes,' I said. 'That's real ice, baby.'
ut as I bent to put my monicker on his ▶

suspender something caught my eye. T
stitching on the flare. It wasn't right. In fact,
was left. It should have been on the right leg
pulled the flare out and examined it. I won't t
you exactly what I saw on the flare until the e
of the story, because that's how you tell storie
holding out on bits of info to keep you gu
interested.

'Just as I thought,' I declared. 'This isn't a re
Max Normal suit. This is mock Leon Brittan. This
fake city, kitty. This is cheap *copyville!*

The young pretender with the suspend
turned and started to run, and I went out afte
He headed off the main drag into a sidestree
But he wasn't going to get away from Mr Norm
I threw my trusty brolly at his feet. He yelped.
tripped. He fell. And the next minute he w
looking into the eyes of one mad Max.

'Okay, Man what gives? Where did you get
the ersatz?'

'I-I'm truly sorrysville, Daddy,' he whimpered
want to be a cool cat like you, but I can't affo
the real fur, you dig my drift? These copies we
going for a pinch. They were cheapsburg, mar

I asked the faker where he bought the cu
suit. He was about open his mouth and tell n
when something strange happened. His mou
didn't open. Instead his eyes started to flick
like, like these crazy flickering eyes. Then h
mouth started to shake, rattle and dribble, ar
then he turned away from me and starte
walking. He was walking slowly, like a zombie, li
a Joe on tow, like a man with a plan that wasn
his own.

Max, baby, I said to myself. I think you've ju
stumbled on something mega.

I followed Johnny Ersatz for about ha
an hour. Eventually we arrived at t
dingy warehouse district of Mega-Cit
next to the commercial spaceport.
now I had little more than one hour to solve th
puzzle and save my show and the inalienab
right of free men to wear flared trousers. Ersa
walked real slow, like a sleepwalker, and finally
came to this warehouse and he knocked thre
times on the door. The door opened, and
walked in. Me, I used my brolly to climb up th
side of the warehouse, then I slipped in cool
you like through a fanlight window. I cre
through a few small rooms and then came in
the main warehouse, where I saw my old frier
Ersatz. Next to Ersatz were about a dozen mo
cats in Max suits, though I guessed that all
these were fakeroonees too. They all had that
now familiar lobotomized look that Ersatz wor

The warehouse was full of boxes. One was open and I saw a stack of imitationville Max Normal pin-striped suits. A few Leon Brittans, a couple of Max Normal Regulars and some Stockbroker 5001s. There was also a stack of computers, and a few thugs with guns. A man was behind the computers, talking to the zombie normals. When he stepped into view it almost blew my mind. For one second my cool began to melt as I recognised that terrible withered frame, that peroxide cropped head, that hideous little face. This was none other than the Godfather of Fashion, the Don of the Rag Trade.

' 'Scarface' Gaultier,' I whispered to myself.

'Scarface' Gaultier, also known as The Frog, was leader of the most vicious fashion mob in Mega-City, but recently I'd been cutting into his profit margin, not to mention his prophet margin. The reds he got from his illicit bicycle shorts sales had been hit by the growing popularity of my normal wear. I should have known The Frog would have been behind the plot to zap me and flared trousers off the map.

He moved some buttons on the computer and a few of the ersatz Normals jerked. They jerked towards one of the crates, where some of Gaultier's jerks handed them a pile of fake normal suits.

'Give them to your friends,' squeaked The Frog. 'In one hour we'll have another little show. I'll hit the right buttons on this lovely little computer and more followers of Max Normal will go on the rampage, and that pigswill don of demode Max Normal will get the blame.'

So that was it. The Normalites were being controlled by Gaultier through the fake suits. I'd seen enough. Carefully I took off my bowler hat where, inside, there was a mini-phone linked directly to Judge Dredd's bike. I pressed the button.

'Dredd.'

'Dredd, baby. Has Max got some fashion facts for you!'

'Spill it, Normal.'

'Scarface Gaultier, daddy. He's the ham behind the scam.'

I gave Dredd directions to the warehouse. And then, as I went to put my bowler hat back on my mat (that's my hair to anyone who's not tuned into Normalspeak) I fumbled. The hat fell through my hands. Are my fingers made out of butter or are they made out of butter? The bowler fell down to the warehouse below. It landed right in front of Gaultier, who looked up and saw me looking down.

Too cool, Maxie, I said to myself. Blown it you most definitely have.

'Normal!' shrieked Scarface.

'Gaultier!' I shrieked back, as I couldn't think of anything chicer to shriek. Next moment I was running towards the fanlight window. All I had to do was avoid Gaultier's cats until Dredd showed his head: but they were coming at me from all sides. Crazy, I thought. Real Little Big Hornville. I reached the fanlight as Scarface's thugs closed in. I leapt up towards it, about to catch the ledge with the edge of my brolly, but at that moment a fat cat in spats knocked me flat. Now I'm a mean ▶

machine when it comes to fighting clean, but this was a really uncool dirty scene. There were ten of them, and the last time I looked there was only one of me. They dragged me down to the warehouse floor and threw me in front of Scarface.

'Freeze out, Scarface,' I said. 'What gives with the Max Attack?'

'I'll tell you what gives, Normal. It's quite simple. I'm going to kill you.'

Hey, a little thing like impending doom and destruction isn't enough to faze the Normal. Even when Gaultier's boys attached me to a large kind of printing press, my cool wasn't blown, my calm wasn't thrown. I knew I had to keep Gaultier rapping. I had to tow the line and play for time. When Dredd turned up everything would be fine.

By the gleam in Gaultier's mean little eyes I figured that he had no normal murder planned.

'What's the score, superbore?' I asked him. 'Are you putting the chap with the knack on the rack?'

'More than that, you garbage-mouthed anachronism,' he replied, pushing down a lever on the printing press. Immediately I started to shiver and vibrate. The press on which I was tied rose.

'This is an old-fashioned tee-shirt printing machine, Normal,' sniggered Scarface. 'I'm going to give you a change of appearance. I'm going to crush you into a *psychedelic tee-shirt*.'

Psychedelic tee-shirt! the thought stuck in my mind like a fishbone in a throat. I began to froth at the mouth, man. I mean, was I rabid or was I a

mad dog? I was lowered down. To my left I sa cartons of ink. Bright blues and reds and yellow

'No use struggling, Normal. How I've longed fo this day. How I've loathed your silly pin-stripe suits, your appalling flares, your excruciating sensible shoes. You stand for everything I mos detest!'

'So sit down, Scarface,' came a deep an familiar voice. It was Dredd. He was standing the door of the warehouse. Well, things got little complicated here. There were shots an shouts and screams. You know the score so won't be a bore. Few minutes later, Dredd ha untied me. He was still fighting off some c Gaultier's boys. Gaultier himself was a weird who had disappeared o.

'Back in a beat, Dredd, baby,' I said, leaping o the printing machine and picking up my bowle from the floor. 'I'm going to play cat and mous with the louse. I'm going to slog the Frog. I' going to assaultier the Gaultier.'

'Just shut up talking about it and do it, Norma grunted Dredd.

'Sure thing, Daddy. I've heard your word.'

Gaultier had slipped out through the fanligh window onto the roof. A few moments later I wa up there with him. He had about a fifty yard sta on me, but his retreat was incomplete: he wa slowed down by his bright yellow baggy trouser with straps joining each leg. What a fashio victim, I said to myself, as I leapt through the a without care, the King of Kool, the Prince of th Pin-Stripes, the Lord of the Ties, the Nawab c Normality.

As I caught up with Scarface he turned to stand his ground. I deftly struck the first blow with my brolly to his rib cage. The pup doubled up.

'You're out of the bout, Scarface,' I said, tipping my hat back. But at that moment Gaultier hit back. From his inside pocket he produced a small bottle and threw the contents in my face. I reeled back. It was expensive French perfume for men. I felt my life flash before my eyes. No Normal would be smelt dead reeking of anything but soap and water.

Before I could recover, The Frog had leapt at me and knocked me off my feet. I lay on my back, looking up at him, as he pulled a revolting expressionistic cravat from his neck. The sunlight glinted on the edges of the cravat as he lifted it above me. The squaresville neckerchief was lined with razors!

'Goodbye, Normal' said the Frog.

Now you might think this was a heavy scene, but it takes more than a cravat attack to tax Max. Gaultier was standing above me, about a yard from the edge of the roof, and I'd already dug that his feet were on the splayed material of my thirty inch flares. As he lifted the razor-cravat I pulled my legs away, and his feet shot up in the air . He let out the old Fashion Mob curse of 'May the suit of Armani be upon you,' and then was over the edge and over the hill.

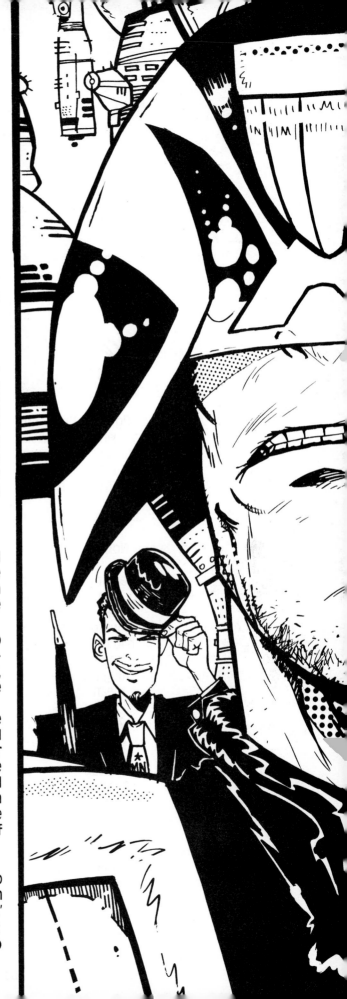

When I got onto street level I found Gaultier lying in a heap. He looked like the sort of meal you get served in cheap chinese restaurants. Dredd drove up on his bike.

'Nice work, Normal. We'll get the medics to patch him up, then we'll throw him in a Crim-Cube. I reckon nine to eleven years. By the way, how was the punk controlling those fake Normals?'

'Easy, Man. There were little mechanisms in the flares of the phoney suits,' I said. (This is what I saw when I first looked at the suspender pretender's mock Leon Brittan chunky pin-stripe flare. Remember?) 'The mechanisms were linked to the computers in the warehouse. When activated I reckon they sent messages to the wearers' brains. And so Gaultier had an army of barmy Normals.'

Dredd revved his bike, about to depart.

'Okay, Normal. You're in the clear. You can go ahead with the Max Normal Mega-City Fashion Show. And your suits will remain legal. For now.'

'Cool, Baby,' I said, tipping my hat. 'You can't say *flarer* than that!'

REAL NAME: JEFF ANDERSON
SOCIAL CATEGORY: ARTIST
STATUS: ACTIVE
CURRENT PROJECT: WILLIAM TELL

FAVOURITE FILMS

1 It's A Wonderful Life
2 Alien
3 Pinocchio
4 Brazil
5 Night Of The Hunter
6 Kind Hearts And Coronets
7 Dead Of Night
8 Son Of Frankenstein
9 The Searchers
10 Spartacus

FAVOURITE TV SHOWS

1 Plays/Film On Four
2 Black Adder
3 Porridge
4 I, Claudius
5 First Tuesday
6 Edge Of Darkness
7 Flay Otters
8 The Addams Family
9 Lost In Space
10 Arena/South Bank Show

FAVOURITE RECORDS

1 Talking Heads: Paper
2 Peter Hamill: My Experience
3 Neil Young: Powderfinger
4 Jerry Harrison: Man With A Gun
5 Talking Heads: Ruby Dear
6 Genesis: Willow Farm
7 Ramones: Swallow My Pride
8 The Pogues: Boys From The County Hell
9 Los Alberto Trios Paranious: Dead Meat
10 David Byrne: What A Day That Was

FAVOURITE COMICS

1 Watchmen
2 Dark Knight
3 Warrior
4 2000 AD
5 Captain Britain
6 TV 21
7 Justice League
8 Anything by Frank Bellamy
9 Anything by John M. Burns
10 Anything by Brian Lewis

FAVOURITE BOOKS

1 Sword At Sunset: Rosemary Sutcliffe
2 Brighton Rock: Graham Greene
3 The Golden Strangers: Henry Treece
4 The Dark Is Rising: Susan Cooper
5 Titus Groan: Mervyn Peake
6 Lord Of The Rings: J.R.R. Tolkien
7 The Maltese Falcon: Dashiell Hammett
8 The Once And Future King: T.H. White
9 To Your Scattered Bodies Go: Philip José Farmer
10 Do Androids Dream Of Electric Sheep: Phillip K. Dick

JUDGE DREDD

BROTHERS 'N' ARMS

TARIQ ALI ALLEY, MEGA-CITY ONE. NIGHT.

'I'VE NEVER KILLED A MAN BEFORE.'

SCRIPT
ALAN GRANT
ART
J. ANDERSON
LETTERING
STELLA

'I'VE NEVER KILLED A WOMAN EITHER. OR A KID. OR EVEN AN ANIMAL. ABOUT ALL I HAVE KILLED IS TIME.'

'FRANKLY, I'D BE MORE THAN HAPPY TO KEEP IT THAT WAY. BUT IT'S MY HANDS, YOU SEE...'

'...THEY'RE GETTING RESTLESS - TWITCHY. AND I'M AFRAID. IF I DON'T GIVE INTO THEM - LET THEM HAVE THEIR EVIL WAY -'

'I COULD BE THE FIRST FATALITY!'

GLURK!

STOP IT! STOP, DAMN YOU! I'VE DONE EVERYTHING YOU WANTED, HAVEN'T I? IT'S NOT MY FAULT IF WE HAVEN'T FOUND YOU A-

-VICTIM.

JUSTICE HQ. THE MED-BAY UNITS.

THE EXTRA ARMS ARE REAL ENOUGH—BUT THEY'RE NOT HIS. THEY'RE *GRAFTS*—NOT EXACTLY A TOP-NOTCH JOB, EITHER. BEATS ME WHY HE'D *WANT* THEM.

FASHION, PROBABLY. THAT'D EXPLAIN THE EXTRA *NAVEL*—AND THE *NIPPLE-NOSES*, TOO!

NAME'S *ERNST EMMINGWY*, FOURTH AVENUE CON-APTS. NO PREVIOUS CRIMINAL FORM—AND WHATEVER ELSE HE IS, *DREDD*, HE'S *NOT* A MUTANT!

BUT IT *DOESN'T* EXPLAIN WHY HE *CHOKED* THE *LIFE* OUT OF SOME POOR SAD!

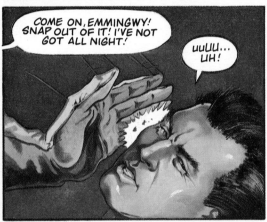

COME ON, EMMINGWY! SNAP OUT OF IT! I'VE NOT GOT ALL NIGHT!

uuUU... UH!

HUH? WHERE—? WHA... WHAT HAPPENED?

YOU TELL *US*! WHY'D YOU STIFF THAT GUY?

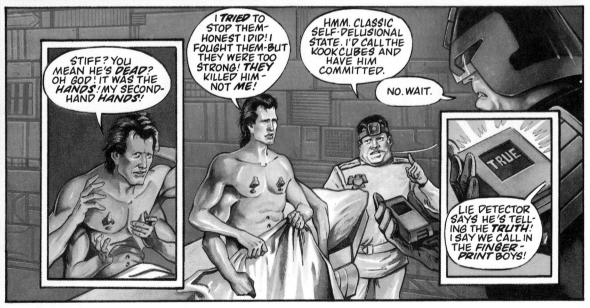

STIFF? YOU MEAN HE'S *DEAD*? OH GOD! IT WAS THE *HANDS*! MY SECOND-HAND *HANDS*!

I *TRIED* TO STOP THEM—HONEST I DID! I FOUGHT THEM—BUT THEY WERE TOO STRONG! *THEY* KILLED HIM—NOT *ME*!

HMM. CLASSIC SELF-DELUSIONAL STATE. I'D CALL THE KOOKCUBES AND HAVE HIM COMMITTED.

NO. WAIT.

TRUE

LIE DETECTOR SAYS HE'S TELLING THE *TRUTH*! I SAY WE CALL IN THE *FINGER-PRINT BOYS*!

WE USE EVERYTHING BUT THE SOUL

RESYK—THE VAST RECYCLING PLANT THAT IS THE FINAL RESTING PLACE FOR OVER TEN MILLION MEGA CITIZENS EVERY YEAR.

1000 CORPSES ARE PROCESSED EVERY HOUR. GUTTED—DISECTED—BROKEN DOWN INTO OVER A HUNDRED USEFUL CONSTITUENTS FOR REUSE IN MEDICINE AND INDUSTRY.

A MONUMENT TO EFFICIENT WASTE-DISPOSAL IN AN AGE WHERE EVERYTHING—INCLUDING HUMAN DIGNITY—IS IN SHORT SUPPLY.

SO WHAT CAN WE DO FOR YOU, JUDGE?

YOU CAN EXPLAIN YOUR SECURITY SET-UP AS REGARDS JUSTICE DEPT-SUPPLIED CORPSES.

SECOND, YOU CAN EXPLAIN HOW THE LIMBS OF A DEMENTED STRANGLER ENDED UP ON THE BLACK ECONOMY GRAFT MARKET!

FINALLY, DEPENDIN' ON YOUR ANSWERS YOU CAN CONSIDER YOURSELF UNDER ARREST!

A-ARREST? B-BUT—?

THAT'S THIRD. START AT FIRST!

UH—AS YOU PROBABLY KNOW, ALL PERPS KILLED IN ACTION COME DIRECTLY IN ON THE SECTOR HOUSE FEEDERS.

CHALLY BURK AND HIS BROTHER DEEZEL ARE THE POLE MEN—THEY KEEP THE BODIES FROM GETTING CAUGHT IN THE MACHINERY.

IF ANYONE KNOWS ABOUT STOLEN LIMBS, THEY'RE THE ONES TO ASK—NOT ME!

THEY'RE ONTO US! *RUN FOR IT!*

STOP IN THE NAME OF THE LAW!

IF WE MAKE FOR THE HI-LEVEL WALKWAY, WE CAN DOUBLE ROUND TO THE REAR EXIT!

HEY, DEEZEL-CHALLY! HOW'S LIFE ON THE PERP LINE? *STIFF GOIN'*, HUH? HAW HAW!

AAAAH!

OUT THE WAY, NEILMAN!

DROKK! *MURDER* NOW!

THAKK!

YOU'RE ONLY MAKIN' THINGS WORSE FOR YOURSELVES! COME DOWN OFF THERE – OR I START *SHOOTIN'*!